ASHFORD
IN OLD PHOTOGRAPHS

Also by Richard Filmer:

Kentish Rural Crafts & Industries
Kent Town Crafts
Hops and Hop Picking
Old Ashford
Ashford in Old Picture Postcards

ASHFORD 1973. A photograph taken over the rooftops of the Lower High Street showing the construction of the new Charter Consolidated office block, much of which is now occupied by Girobank. The building was the largest ever constructed in the town centre and met with much opposition from the people of Ashford. The North Downs can be seen in the background.

ASHFORD
IN OLD PHOTOGRAPHS

COLLECTED BY
RICHARD FILMER

ALAN SUTTON
1988

Alan Sutton Publishing Limited
Brunswick Road · Gloucester

First published 1988

British Library Cataloguing in Publication Data

Ashford in old photographs.
1. Kent. Ashford, history
I. Filmer, Richard
942.2′392

ISBN 0-86299-522-1

Typesetting and origination by
Alan Sutton Publishing Limited.
Printed in Great Britain by
WBC Print Limited.

INTRODUCTION

Ashford has ancient origins. The area was known to the Romans as they forded the river at this point, and today Beaver Road and Station Road run along the route of the Roman Road from Lympne to Canterbury.

The Anglo-Saxon name for the town was Essetesford, which can perhaps be rougly interpreted as 'the fording place on the bend of the river Stour where the ash trees stood'. The town is included in the Domesday Book, which also mentions the church, priest and two mills.

The town was first granted the privilege of holding a market as early as the thirteenth century and over the last century the cattle market has grown into one of the largest in southern England.

By the seventeenth century Camden described Ashford as 'A town of note', and in 1762 another writer's description was 'A pretty and well built town'. However, Nathaniel Spencer, just a few years later wrote that the town was 'Of considerable repute in former times although it has now fallen into decay', yet by 1808 E.W. Brayley stated that Ashford was a 'respectable market and post town'.

Agriculture has been important in the area. Corn and sheep were common commodities, as were hops, clover, timber and underwood. Chestnut-coppiced underwood is still grown within about a mile of the town centre and until the great hurricane of 1987, cherry orchards could be found even closer to the town. From the land, clay was extracted to produce good quality bricks, roof tiles and drainage pipes and other extraction industries included gravel, ragstone and sand.

The greatest influence on the town, until recent years, was the decision by the South Eastern Railway Company to build the Railway Works. In 1841, before the great factory was constructed, the population of the town was not much more than 3,000. By 1851 it had risen rapidly to over 5,000 and it was said that 3,000 Ashford people were dependent upon the railway, inclusive of the workers' families.

Ashford had been a manufacturing town of some note, but until the coming of the railway, most manufacture was for local needs, or related to agriculture. The Ashford tannery was already producing leather in the sixteenth century, an industry that survived until the late 1950s. Over the last century or so, trades and occupations have been wide and varied, including linen manufacture, candle production, rope making, wire working, muffin making, clay smoker's pipe production and even ferret farming.

Society and demands have changed. More changes are to come. In the late 1980s the Channel Tunnel project has applied more pressure on the area than ever before. Most of the traditional trades and industries have been lost. Nevertheless, we still have a large firm of wheelwrights, a flour mill, iron foundries, wool staplers and a market. However, the great railway factory is now closed, although the wheelshop has survived into the 1980s.

It is immediately apparent from the illustrations that there have been striking changes within the town centre and those in the last twenty years or so have been the most dramatic. Gone are those old familiar Ashford business names of Lee & Sons, Knowles & Co., Dixons, Stanhays, Rabsons, Thompsons, Giles, Crameris, James & Kither, Lewis & Hyland and so on.

Although a few old favourite illustrations have been included, some attempt has been made to avoid photographs that have appeared in previous publications. Some of the photographs are rare, but faded, and it is hoped that this will not detract too much from their intrinsic interest. Perhaps surprisingly, photographs from the early part of the century are often more common than those taken within the last thirty years or so.

In spite of the destruction of so many of the town's buildings, one need not look too far to discover its history. It can still be found in the surviving buildings, a number of which can even now be readily identified from the illustrations. Although they are frequently heavily disguised by modern shop fronts, they often reveal a wealth of information about Ashford life in the past and help us understand the development and the needs of the town in days gone by.

ASHFORD PARISH CHURCH. The Ashford Parish Church of St Mary's stands in the very heart of the town. Cruciform in shape it was largely rebuilt by Sir John Fogge in 1470. With its 121ft. tower and 10 bells it was a landmark for miles around. Inside is Sir John's tomb, together with his helmet which weighs nearly 24lb. A late nineteenth century illustration.

THE CATHOLIC CHURCH. The first 'Parish Priest' was Revd James Darell, who served from 1769 to 1775 at the Darell's Chapel in Cale Hill House, Little Chart. The early Ashford Roman Catholic congregations held their meetings at the Prince of Orange public house in New Street – a little ironical insomuch as the Prince of Orange was the Defender of the Protestant faith.

In 1854, Doctor O'Toole from Cale Hill began a fund raising project for the new church, which was opened on 22 August 1865. The architect was Edwin Pugin, son of Augustus Pugin the Gothic revivalist, and the new church was built in the modern Gothic style. The church is dedicated to St Teresa of Avila, although the present Sanctuary and altar were not added until 1892.

THE CEMETERY LODGE and gates photographed in the 1860s. The cemetery still evokes a sense of the Victorian past. Opened in 1859, it was for some decades a favourite place for Ashfordians to take a Sunday afternoon stroll to improve their knowledge of architecture, funerary sculpture and arboriculture. The carefully planned walks were lined with fine specimen trees including some beautiful deodars and the grounds were still peaceful and perhaps, surprisingly, not melancholy.

SADLY THE HURRICANE of October 1987 damaged many of the fine mature trees and caused damage to the sculpture and gravestones. The original Victorian cast-iron railings were restored and replaced in the boundary wall in 1988.

HIGH STREET AND MIDDLE ROW. Perhaps the most photographed spot in Ashford is the view between the High Street and Middle Row across to the impressive 121ft. Kentish ragstone tower of the Parish Church. Stevenson's fish shop has been redeveloped, but the other buildings remain. c. 1935.

ABOVE: Looking down North Street towards Bybrook.
BELOW: Looking east across Station Road, or Marsh Street as it was then known. The row of uniform houses on the right is Linden Road.

ABOVE: Looking north over the lower High Street. The tall building in the centre foreground was the London and County Bank. It is now rebuilt and is the High Street branch of the National Westminster Bank, successors to London & County Bank.

BELOW: Looking west over the top of Bank Street into the upper High Street. The building that can just be seen at the bottom left was the Post Office, later National Provincial Bank (now National Westminster Bank). Barrow Hill Place can be seen at top centre and just to the left, the white-topped cowls of the hop-drying oast can just be detected.

THE LOWER HIGH STREET in the early 1950s. The High Street was one of the widest in Kent –
some 120ft. across at its widest point. Some local historians believe that the lower High
Street was even wider in earlier times. A cattle market was held here until 1856. In those days
the cattle, pigs and sheep, would often roam freely into the shops, to the great
inconvenience of the shopkeepers.

Whilst there have been great changes to the lower end of the south side, the north side is
largely unchanged, although only a few of the shops now use awnings. The road, now
'one-way', has been severely restricted by the recent scheme of widening the pavement.
However, this has enabled the stall market to operate again on Tuesdays and Fridays.

Double-decker buses are now a rare sight.

HIGH STREET in the late 1950s. An interesting photograph looking west which is fascinating to compare with the illustration of the same scene taken a few years earlier on p. 12 looking east. A much needed pedestrian crossing, complete with Belisha beacons, has been introduced. The old Co-op clock was most useful insomuch as the church clock could not be seen from street level in this part of the High Street. On the left is C.F. Hutson's grocery shop, next is Murdoch's radio shop (which later became Globe Wallpapers) and the Bon-Bon Snack Bar, which at that time was still serving 'High Teas'. Just beyond the bus is Fendalls, wine merchants, which later became Scott & Kendon, estate agents and surveyors, who at the time were at 38 High Street opposite.

The very popular Ashford Odeon, which was frequently filled to capacity in those days, was showing *The Big Lift*, starring Montgomery Clift and Kirk Douglas.

In the right foreground can be seen the sign of the Ideal Hairdressing Saloon, which still trades from the same address in the 1980s. In 1916, gentlemen's haircutting was 4*d*. (less than 2p), shaving 2*d*. (less than 1p), whilst ladies haircutting was 6*d*. (2½p) and shampooing 1*s*. (5p). Face massage and scalp massage was 2*s*. (10p).

THE PREMISES OF HUNTER the tailor, hatter and hosier at 64–66 High Street c. 1890, soon after Mr George Harrison Hunter took over John Taylor's outfitter. The photograph is taken from an upper window of Kings Parade opposite. Bayley & Sons the Auctioneers and Valuers occupied part of 66 High Street.

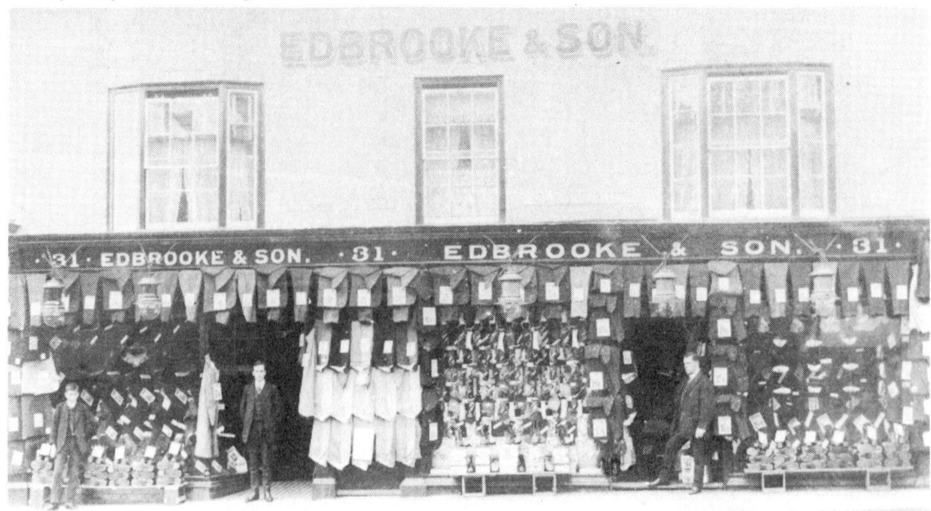

EDBROOKE & SON, 31 High Street, with a crammed window display. The firm occupied the premises from before 1890 until the 1940s. The premises were once an inn with the unusual name of 'The Ounces Head' and were also, for many years, occupied by Scott & Kendon, later to merge with Halifax Estate Agents.

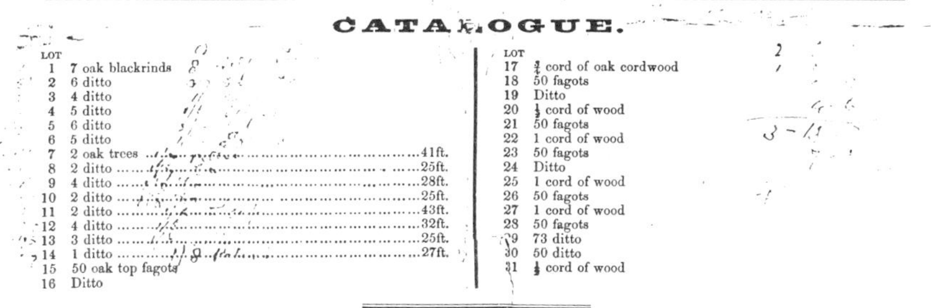

A POSTER PRINTED BY THOMPSON the Ashford printer. Bayleys from 66 High Street specialised in auctioning standing timber and were also cabinet makers. In those days the timber auctions were often held on site in the wood.

MIDDLE ROW and the High Street. With the exception of the Saracen's Head Hotel, the other buildings remain intact. For many years the balconies with their attractive cast iron railings, one over the door of the Saracen's Head Hotel and the other over the butchers forecourt, were favourite pitches for speakers at election time. Some old Ashfordians can remember the days when there were two speakers competing with each other at the same time and many suffering the indignity of eggs being thrown from the cheering and jeering crowd down on the street.

THE SARACEN'S HEAD HOTEL stood on the corner of the High Street and the west side of North Street; an inn with a long history – certainly in existence in 1478, but dramatically reconstructed and enlarged along North Street in 1862. In the 1850s the Magistrates held sittings at the inn on the first Saturday of the month.

THE INN WAS TOTALLY DEMOLISHED in 1967 and the new Sainsbury's supermarket, built by Messrs Epps, was constructed. Boots took over the building when Sainsbury's later supermarket was opened in Park Street.

MARKS & SPENCER, 64–66 High Street, previously G.H. Hunter & Co. Ltd Outfitters. The premises were redeveloped in the mid-1930s by Marks & Spencer and was built in the precise 'modern' style of the period. On the left is The George Hotel and on the right Boots – later remodelled as Barclays Bank.

THE MIDDLE HIGH STREET. Although the photograph was taken as recently as 1965, none of the shops illustrated are still trading in the same position. The street seems remarkably traffic-free considering that the Ring Road had not been completed.

HIGH STREET nos. 105, 107 and 109, photographed in 1973, shortly before the premises were demolished to form the Tufton Centre. Fosters, the outfitters, occupied the premises of 105 High Street, once occupied by Crameri's. The handsome building in the centre was a chemist shop for nearly 150 years, the last chemist being Mr Marks. Next door was Warner the butcher. Castle Street is in the foreground.

PILCHER'S SHOE SHOP (established 1849) closing down sale. There have been a remarkable number of shoe shops in the town for many years and out of a row of five shops illustrated here, three were shoe retailers.

HIGH STREET nos. 84/86. Messrs F.W. Woolworth & Co. Bazaar, as it was then known, was established on its present site in about 1928. The frontage expanded over the years and in the mid-1950s the old premises, occupied for many decades by Pilcher's Boot & Shoe shop were acquired and demolished together with Chamber's Garage at the rear in Park Street. The premises were totally rebuilt in yellow brick, although the shop did not close for a single working day whilst it was being redeveloped.

THE UPPER HIGH STREET in the early 1930s. The dominant building on the right is 89–91 High Street, a building with a most satisfying Georgian elevation in which, years ago, the Hyland and Startup families resided. In about 1900 Mr H.A.C. Abell rented a room at No. 89 to run the Accident Assurance Company, which in 1906 was taken over by the Commercial Union Assurance Co. They eventually took the whole of the building, which in 1930 was considered to be the largest and most up-to-date office in Ashford.

In the early 1980s the building was demolished but the facade was rebuilt in identical style.

UPPER HIGH STREET. A favourite card by the Ashford photographer, De'Ath. Both the Castle Hotel and the restaurant on the left advertise 'Good accommodation for cyclists', indicating the popularity of cycling in the earlier years of the century.

Sole Agents for GENT'S "SPECIAL BECTIVE." 16/6

HORTON'S SHOE SHOP at 96–98 High Street. The business was founded in 1837 by Henry Horton and remained in the family for four generations until it was sold to 'K' Shoes in 1966. This shop front was installed in 1900 by the Ashford builder, E.J. Bowles.

BEVAN'S GENERAL DRAPERS AND OUTFITTERS STORES at 70, 72 and 74 High Street. No. 70 & 72 later became Timothy Whites and Taylors, chemists and hardware merchants and, in 1987, the premises were redeveloped for Messrs W.H. Smith's new shop. 74 High Street became Burtons, the tailors.

The narrow passage between 72 and 74 leading into Park Street still survives. It is called Taylor's Passage after John Taylor, draper, who occupied the adjoining premises from around 1860.

HIGH STREET nos. 74 & 76. In the early 1930s Messrs Montague Burton remodelled the premises previously occupied by Hugh Bevan, the Ashford draper. At the time it was one of the most architecturally modern buildings in the town. Note the glazed finish to the upper storey, with the pillared effect between the windows and the geometric pattern over. This style of architecture dates from the 1920s but did not reach Ashford until 10 years later.

ONE OF THE FINEST SURVIVING BUILDINGS in the town is perhaps the outstanding late seventeenth-century building on the corner of North Street and High Street (now Burtons). From the 1880s until about 1904, this prominent shop was occupied by Thomas Coulthard, linen draper, silk mercer, milliner, tailor and habit maker.

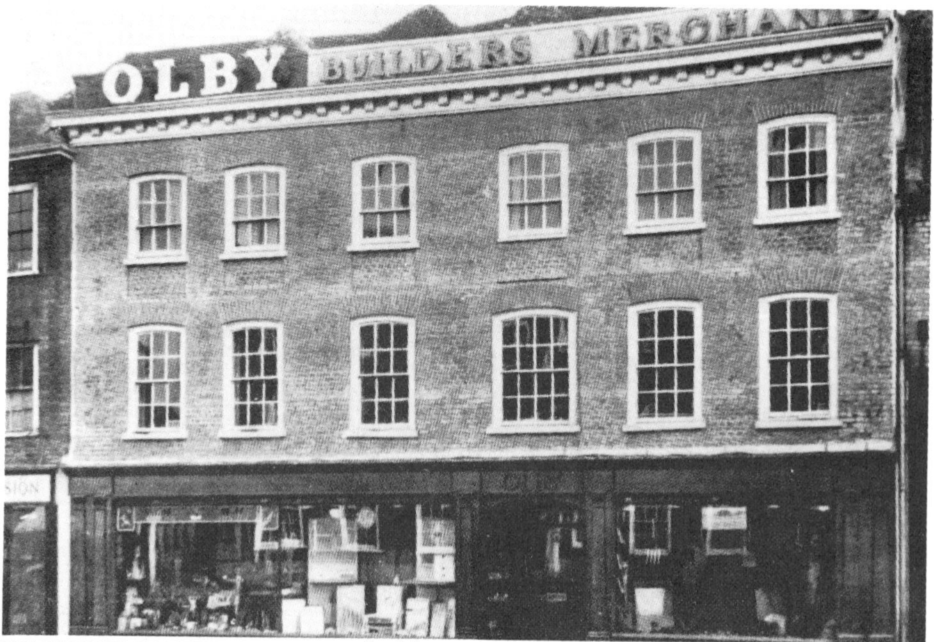

THE PREMISES OF ALFRED OLBY LIMITED, builders merchants and iron-mongers, at 5 High Street. They occupied the premises from about 1936 until the building was demolished in 1970. It was previously the Royal Oak Inn, where once the sale of corn took place, at one time occupied by Lee & Son, furnishers.

HIGH STREET nos. 27, 29 and 31. The photograph dates from about 1960. For many years the Candy Store was Jenner's, the pastry cook. Shortly after the photograph was taken, the building was remodelled as Gizzi's Restaurant.

RABSON'S SHOP at 55 High Street photographed in the 1950s. Note the exciting window display, which delighted Ashford children when the store was run by Mr Cue during the 1950s and '60s. In the seventeenth century, the premises were the 'Six Bells Inn'. The Rabsons have traded in the town since 1720 and Mr Donald Rabson continued his watch and clock business until 1987.

MIDDLE ROW. A rare photograph, c. 1910, looking up Middle Row. The banner advertises Passmore's Restaurant and Dining Rooms at 51 and 53 High Street, next to Rabsons' old shop, which served the town from the turn of the century until about 1950. The architecture is typical of the local Kentish style with good use of traditional local materials – the soft red local bricks, Kent peg tiles, Kent ragstone footings and ragstone road surface worn smooth by generations of feet and horses. Apart from the building in the immediate foreground most of the other buildings on the left remain reasonably intact.

NORTH STREET AND HIGH STREET JUNCTION. An illustration probably from the 1930s. Traffic lights had not arrived and at the time a pair of convex mirrors, illuminated by the lamppost, seemed to deal with traffic problems at this busy junction, enabling motorists to observe what was happening 'round the corner'.

A PRE-FIRST WORLD WAR photographic postcard looking down the wide High Street. A market was held in this part of the High Street until 1856 and in the 1980s, now the pavements have been widened, the Tuesday and Friday stall market has been reintroduced.

LEE AND SON dates back to 1868 when Mr Frederick Lee commenced business at 4 High Street (side), now demolished. Further premises were acquired in the town, including 30 High Street (seen above), the Royal Oak (later Olby's), together with premises in Wellesley Road and Station Road.

THE FURLEY FOUNTAIN. An excellent pre-1900 illustration of the handsome drinking fountain that was built on the site of the old town pump in the High Street. It was erected, at his own cost, by the well-known historian, a solicitor and one time Undersheriff to the County, Robert Furley, father of Sir John Furley.

STATION ROAD (then known as Marsh Street) photographed at the turn of the century. The ivy covered building in the left foreground is St John's House, the original Cottage Hospital. The only remaining building today is the Baptist Church, built by W. Fowler in 1881.

ALTHOUGH ONLY PHOTOGRAPHED in the early 1970s, nothing remains today. Every single building illustrated was demolished for the new Ring Road. The scene is the junction of the lower High Street and East Hill with a turning right into Station Road. Hoskins tobacconists and Tiffany's cafe have already closed; the demolition contractor's board indicates that demolition work is about to start.

NORWOOD STREET. A faded illustration of Norwood Street looking towards Queen Street. Messrs W. & T. Avery took over the workshops of Goulden & Wind, the pianoforte manufacturers, in about 1904 and remained in the street until the late 1960s. Before the use of the pneumatic drill, roadworks were a most labour intensive task – using a remarkable number of men and a vast array of hand tools.

NEW STREET now forms the link road from Magazine Road roundabout to the Ring Road and in Victorian times was a street of some commercial importance, with a most impressive list of craftsmen and tradesmen. For example, in 1845, the wide variety included Thomas Burton and James Howland, both boot and shoe makers, Joseph Davis, the rope maker, Mrs Frances Down, straw bonnet maker, William Fairbrass, the cooper, John Hill, the millwright, William and Thomas Humphrey, coach builders (who, along with the shopkeeper John Vile, were licensed to hire horses), Joy Cooper, the stonemason, Edward Lacey, the blacksmith, William Robinson, the dyer, John Snelling, the watchmaker and John Tindall, the wireworker.

Other shopkeepers in New Street at this period included butchers, fruiterers, a number of beer, ale and wine retailers, together with many public houses.

Just a few of the houses on the left still survive, together with the British Volunteers Inn.

NEW STREET C. 1960. The Catholic Church can just be seen on the left but with the exception of the Prince Albert and the Prince of Orange public houses (the latter hardly discernible centre right), every other building illustrated has been demolished to form the Magazine Road roundabout.

NEW STREET, LOOKING WEST, in the late 1950s. In the left foreground is Mr Collins' Tank Milk Bar, which later became an Indian restaurant. To the right of Gouldens was Scotts secondhand Bargain Shop.

THE CEDARS PHOTOGRAPHED IN VICTORIAN TIMES. The Cedars, situated on the corner of Elwick Road and Church Road, is one of the most distinctive buildings in the area. It was built in the grand Victorian tradition with a shallow pitched slate roof, ornamental reticulated and dressed stone, an impressive porch with balcony over and a lovely ornate conservatory.

The house was originally occupied in the 1860s by the Elliotts (booksellers and watchmakers of Middle Row, predecessors of Thompson, see p. 65) and then from 1913 by Frederick Hyland, of Lewis & Hylands, who had previously resided at 91 High Street.

Croquet was played on the carefully maintained lawn. Well-dressed figures sit in the garden and even the man mowing the lawn appears to be wearing a top hat. From 1941 the premises were occupied by Ashford Urban District Council, where the Clerk and Treasurer's Department were housed.

In 1980 the Ashford Borough Council applied for planning consent to demolish the building, together with others in Elwick Road, to build the new Civic Centre. Planning consent was refused and the Civic Centre was eventually built in Tannery Lane. The building is situated within a designated conservation area.

BANK STREET, nos. 11–13 the offices of Hallett & Co. solicitors, photographed in the 1950s. The firm was founded by Robert Furley, who opened an office in New Rents in 1830. The following year he moved his office to 30 North Street where he then lived. In 1855 the firm was known as Furley Hallett and Creery and moved to the Bank Street premises in about 1880. In 1955 the firm's title changed to Hallett & Co. Note the window flower-boxes which, until recently, were old wartime ammnunition boxes. The part of the premises on the left, shown occupied by Royal Insurance (and at one time occupied by Richardsons, see p. 62) is also now part of Hallett & Co.'s office.

NEW STREET. An illustration dating from 1973. The British Volunteers Inn still survives, although the inn sign has been replaced. The building to the right, together with Mrs Perkins' grocery shop on the far right, has been demolished to make way for a car sales area.

HEMPSTED STREET in 1973. A street now destroyed to make way for the Tufton Centre. The fascinating street once housed the Friends Meeting House, a herring hang for smoking kippers over oak shavings, the Wellesley and the Coach & Horses public houses, the St Augustine's Academy School, the Domino Stores and Danns secondhand shop. The street was originally known as Drum Lane, the building on the corner of Hempsted Street and New Rents being the Drum Inn.

NORTH STREET in the early 1970s — a dramatic photograph taken through a broken window of a building soon to be demolished. Most of the buildings on the left have been restored. The Army Careers Information Office became Ashford Book Shop, whilst Sercombes Outfitters, previously of Middle Row, took the adjoining property.

The site used as a car park opposite has been redeveloped. This ancient route out of the town is no longer a through road and the area became pedestrianised in the mid-1980s.

NORTH STREET, no. 7. For many years the premises of Mr Price the Opthalmic Optician. Over the top window in the gable the date 1671 is clearly carved, although the building was originally constructed in the previous century. The brick building to the left, once the offices of Ashford Urban District Council, was demolished for the widening of Park Street.

THE FAMILIAR SIGN OF BURNAGE projecting from Burnage's shop at 30 North Street could be seen later at the shop at 22 Bank Street. During World War I Mr Burnage travelled the district on a Douglas motor cycle, tuning pianos. He opened the North Street shop in the 1890s and later moved to 82 High Street (now Woolworths), and around 1922 moved on to 22 Bank Street.

MR HERBERT BURNAGE photographed in 1933. As a choir boy he sang solo for the Prince of Wales and later his voice was trained under Sir Henry Wood. He was a keen musician and provided a number of popular operas and musical events at the Corn Exchange, which were an enormous success.

BURNAGE'S SHOP at 82 High Street. For the King's Wembley Speech of 1924, Mr Burnage provided loud speakers in the shop to enable the people of Ashford, who did not have radios, to have the opportunity of listening to His Majesty.

NORTH STREET. The Somerset Arms can be seen in the centre left on the corner of North Street and Somerset Road, which was demolished for the Ring Road. The shop in the left foreground is 52 and 54 North Street (now demolished for Ashdown Court flats) and was for many years the premises of the Joint Stock Bakery.

The Alfred Joint Stock Company was established back in 1854 in the days of the Crimean War and was originally known as the Alfred Joint Stock Bread and Flour Company. Their early advertisements claimed that their bread and flour was sold at 'lowest possible prices', and their North Street Bakery was 'always open to inspection'. Being a Joint Stock company, customers participated in their declared bonus. In 1924 the bonus paid during the previous 15 years was £39,205.

The bakery, with its side-flue ovens, was situated in the basement of the North Street premises, which were damaged by an incendiary bomb during the last war. In fact a number of bakeries in the Ashford area suffered bomb damage – the Co-op Bakery in Victoria Crescent, Snashalls Bakery in Kent Avenue and another smaller bakery in Godinton Road. Many of the bakeries helped each other out by providing oven space.

One of the best-known managers of the Joint Stock Bakery was Mr Bennett, who ran the business on a strict army-type routine and lived over the premises.

A WARTIME PHOTOGRAPH of one of the company's vans delivering hot cross buns. The vans were immaculately maintained in their maroon and cream livery with gold lettering. The driver is Bill Pemble. The young man standing is Ron Pemble the driver's mate. Stale bread was carried on top of the vehicle and used for pig food.

UNTIL THE END OF THE SECOND WORLD WAR four horse-drawn vans still delivered in the urban area. This is Horace Cook photographed in Jemmett Road. The horses were stabled at the rear of the North Street premises.

HENRY HEADLEY'S GROCERY SHOP at 46 High Street photographed in 1892. Mr Headley established his grocery wholesale and retail business in 1848. By the time the firm was celebrating its centenary it had a number of branches in Ashford (one of the earliest, 1858, being the Alfred Stores at Newtown) and the suburbs, together with village stores. Henry Headley died in 1909 aged 85 and the business continued through his son Mr L.P. Headley, and his grandson Mr L.W. Headley who, in later years, was assisted by his son Mr M.L. Headley, thus continuing the firm through four generations until 1981. In the late 1970s the premises were demolished and the façade was rebuilt in the same style using the original materials. The shop is now in the hands of Headley Brothers, whose directors are also great-grandsons of the original Mr Henry Headley. The redevelopment merged 44 and 46 High Street, now together as 44.

HUTSON'S GROCERS SHOP in the High Street, fondly remembered by Ashfordians as the last of the town's high class grocers. The shop was occupied by John Worger from the early nineteenth century and later by Sankeys, who held the Royal Warrant for supplying the Duke of Edinburgh from Eastwell Park. Sadly the shop closed in 1974 and became a Wimpy Bar.

FOR OVER THIRTY YEARS the business was run on very traditional lines by Mr A.G. Morris, left, and his son-in-law Mr C.E. Raynes. He specialised in fine foods, with a range of over sixty varieties of cheeses.

CRUMPS THE GROCERS opened in Bank Street in 1929 and in the 1930s took over the premises of 41 and 43 High Street, latterly occupied by C. Moakes, pastry cook's and tea rooms. Coming from Folkestone, Mr Crump was so impressed with the recently built Odeon there that he decided to completely redevelop the premises in the then fashionable 'Odeon' style and at the period the premises were described as 'the last word in modernity'.

THE INTERIOR OF THE SHOP was also planned on clean, sleek lines and was one of the first grocers to provide rails for resting shoppers' bags on. The premises now house the Midland Bank.

IN THOSE DAYS most local shopkeepers provided a delivery service and errand boys on their bicycles were a common sight in the town until the 1960s. Local businessman, Mr Sonny Hanson, who owned the New Street fish and chip shop, took a great deal of interest in the affairs of the town and organised the Errand Boys Derby which was usually held in Carnival Week. The illustration shows Crump's boy to be the winner. He is proudly wearing a huge rosette and holding the prize cup.

MIDDLE ROW, No. 4, photographed in 1957 when occupied by Barkers. This interesting timber-framed building dates back to the sixteenth century. Note the intricately carved barge boards to the gable and the Victorian supporting columns to the balcony. One well-known occupant was E.G. Waghorne the butcher. The Phoenix firemark which is clearly visible in the gable has now been restored and moved to a more prominent position.

THE INTERNATIONAL STORES, or the International Tea Company as it was then known, arrived in Ashford in around 1880 at 103 High Street. At the turn of the century their premises were taken over by Leonard Burch, the electrician and cycle maker. They moved over the road to 92 High Street in about 1902 (illustrated above). The premises were redeveloped in about 1960. The company remained on the site until it was redeveloped again in the 1980s for Park Mall shopping precinct.

LIPTON'S SHOP was on the corner of Bank Street and Tufton Street in premises previously occupied by Mrs Amy Howland, the fruiterer. After Liptons closed in about 1960, the shop was taken over by Nicholas Kingsman, the bakers. Since then there have been many changes.

JOHN HOWLAND'S BUSINESS opened at 12 Bank Street in the 1860s and the illustration dates back to the 1870s. The business was obviously successful for by 1887 the firm also occupied premises at 2A Bank Street, 105 High Street and Norwood Street, together with adjoining premises at 14 Bank Street. Apart from the grocery and wine trade the firm were also wholesale tea dealers and manufacturing confectioners, one of their specialities being the 'Howlands Cough Lozenge'. Their steam confectionery works originally operated from 12 and 14 Bank Street and by 1895 they also had a jam factory in Tufton Street. No. 12 Bank Street became Gizzi's in the late 1950s.

THE TRADITIONAL BUTCHER has almost become a thing of the past in recent years. One of the last of the traditional butchers was Sellers of 13 New Street, on the corner of Gilbert Road, which had been a butcher's shop for many years. J.A. Sellers took over the business in 1938 from John Hooker and it was continued by his two sons, Ken and Roy.

In the 1930s a refrigerator was installed by the Lightfoot Refrigeration Co. and the installers had to sleep in the premises overnight. Whilst sleeping on top of the refrigerator they turned on the motor to provide a little heat. Evidently it was turned on too quickly for the heat turned the cement floor to red and the refrigerator became known as the only one to have a red floor. During the war the refrigerator failed and Messrs Stanhay & Co., the local engineers, made a temporary repair by taking the piston from an Austin Seven to make the compressor work. The part remained installed for many years to come. Now, the parts, complete with the Austin Seven piston, form part of the Lightfoot Refrigeration Company's Museum.

After trading as a butcher's shop for most of the century, the business finally closed in 1987.

Left to right, Bill Reeves (previously the Kingsnorth Road butcher), Ken Sellers and Roy Sellers. The shop was the last butchers in Ashford to have sawdust on the floor and the staff wore horizontally striped fleshers' aprons.

JACK GUY'S WELL-KNOWN PORK BUTCHER'S SHOP at 3 Castle Street.

JOHN EDWARD PACKHAM, pork butcher at 65 High Street. He was in business from the 1880s through to the 1920s.

GEORGE CARTER'S PORK BUTCHER'S SHOP at 13 Middle Row, later Flinns cleaners. George Carter was also a fruiterer and the premises claimed to be the original sausage and tripe factory. The shop later became Scotts Dyers (see p. 9).

ASHFORD CO-OPERATIVE SOCIETY. It was during lunchtime on the 4 May 1926 that fire broke out at the Co-op in the lower High Street. The Ashford Fire Brigade attended and, as a contemporary report stated, 'Worked splendidly and heroically' to stop the fire. It was a difficult task as there was a wind driving the fire towards the rear of the premises where access was restricted because of the congestion of properties in the area.

The Co-op opened in the town in 1887, originally at Hempsted Street and by 1895 at 24 High Street. It soon had two further branches at 49 and 152 Beaver Road, together with another branch at Cudworth Road, South Willesborough, and their coal wharf at the LCD railway station.

Less than two years after the High Street fire, huge crowds attended the opening of what became known as the New Central Premises, which was fitted out with quality walnut counters and display cases. On the first floor there was an oak-panelled assembly hall capable of seating nearly 300 people and on the second floor a caretaker's flat.

THE NEW CENTRAL CO-OP PREMISES just after the 1928 rebuilding. In comparison to the great depth of the shop (some 210ft.) the frontage was comparatively narrow. However, the architect overcame the problem of providing sufficient window display for the many departments by arranging an island window with the wide windows cutting back inside the shop in the form of an arcade.

DIXONS

of ASHFORD

ALBION HOUSE, 7 Middle Row, now part of the Man of Kent public house, will probably be for ever remembered by older Ashfordians as Dixons the Ironmongers. In the 1860s Mark Farmer occupied the shop as a linen draper and it then became a tailor's shop. In the 1870s Tatham & Darracot were the first ironmongers and tool dealers to occupy the premises — a trade that was to continue for a century.

THE BUSINESS WAS TAKEN-OVER by Allens in the 1890s who, apart from being hardware dealers, also made cycles. The illustration from the early days of Dixons, who occupied the premises from about 1900, indicates a particularly wide range of lines being sold in the shop.

HIGH STREET, Nos. 32 and 34. In 1912 Thomas Morris Turner took over the jewellery, silversmiths and watchmakers business at 32 and 34 High Street. The trade had been carried on at the premises since the 1830s and had at one time been run by Edward Hayward another well-known watchmaker and jeweller. The business passed to T.M. Turner's son, Benjamin Turner (known as Archie) who was also known for being a founder member of the re-formed Ashford Cricket Club after World War I and is seen in the photograph standing outside the door of No. 32.

During the depression of the 1930s the premises were reduced to No. 32 only and in the 1930s the large competing firm of James Walker opened smart new premises opposite. Trade declined and the firm finally closed in about 1938. One of Benjamin's sons, Robert Turner, took up the trade and joined James Walker in 1950 and became Manager.

LEWIS & HYLANDS MAIN SHOP in New Rents. The tall central building was built by the Ashford builder H. Knock. At one time, apart from the parish church, this was the tallest building in the town. Part of the site was once part of the grounds occupied by the Friends Meeting House.

ASHFORD SHOPKEEPERS often took great pride in their window displays and a window dressing competition, usually held in October, was a popular event.

Wright Brothers 38 British (a name that remained in the town until the mid-1980s), won third prize in 1912. Mr S.J. Linkins, who helped with the display, is standing on the right.

PEARSON BROTHERS of 54 High Street, (later Burtons, see p. 23) were famed for the presentation of their windows in Edwardian times. Perhaps one of their most skilful novelty displays was a model of Ashford Church made up entirely of white linen handkerchiefs, which won first prize in 1906.

FRANK PALMER'S OUTFITTERS SHOP at 111–113 High Street on the corner of Hempsted Street. This superb photograph clearly shows overcoats with caped shoulders, almost highwayman's style and priced at 4s. 11d., moleskin jackets, turned inside out with the check showing, at 3s. 11d. together with a good supply of leather end braces. The premises were demolished to form the High Street frontage of the Tufton Centre.

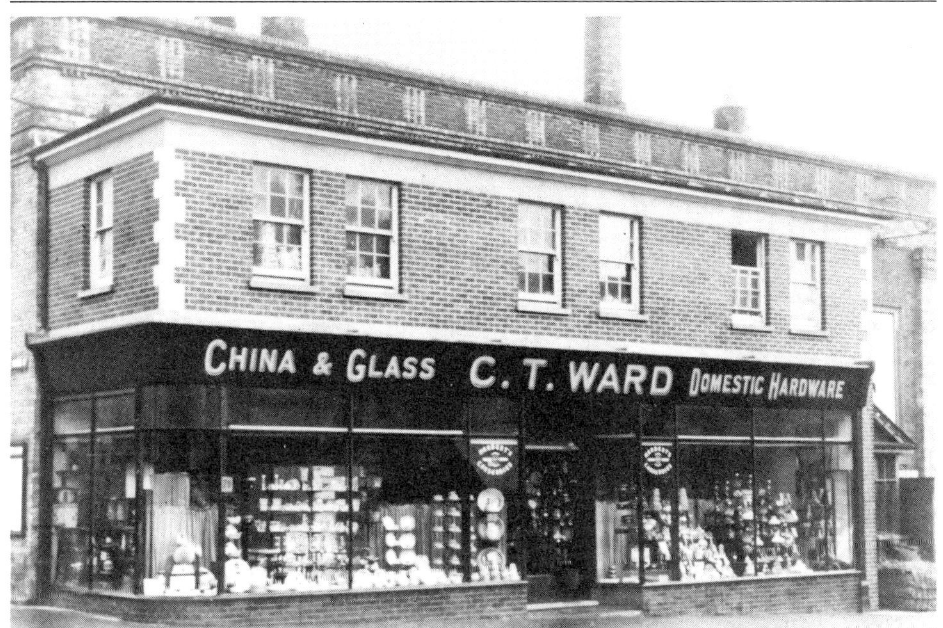

IN 1926 MR CHARLES WARD, previously Secretary to Messrs Burnage Epps, established his china, glass and hardware business in a brand new shop, built by Messrs C.I. Epps, abutting the Corn Exchange. By 1934 the firm became known as Ward & Moore and later, after the war, Mr Humphreys went into partnership. The firm became Ward & Humphreys and continued until 1966, when the premises were demolished.

ANOTHER WELL-KNOWN CHINA SHOP was Giles of 30 Bank Street. Mr Giles moved to the Bank Street shop in about 1876. He continued to visit the shop daily for many years and in 1938, at the age of 96, was the oldest living retail china and glass dealer in the UK. In the 1970s, just before the shop finally closed, Mr Giles' son, grandson and great-grandson, were all serving in the shop.

GEORGE WRAIGHT KNOWLES opened up a business in about 1856 in Regents Place, where he made feather beds and also carried on the oddly allied business of ginger beer making (made to a secret recipe). Both the ginger beer and feather beds were delivered to customers by Mr Knowles in a horse-drawn van and, on the return journey in rural areas, feathers were brought back to his workshops.

In 1863 additional premises were opened at 113 High Street (later Frank Palmer's) for the sale of furniture and bedding. Ten years later he moved across the road to 106 High Street.

Later, further premises were acquired on both sides of Castle Street. By the time the firm celebrated its centenary in 1963 they had over 16,000sq.ft. of showrooms, for furniture, fabrics, floor coverings, baby carriages, domestic electrics, radio and television; together with workshops where skilled craftspeople repolished, upholstered, restored furniture, made curtains, pelmets, etc., and there was also a removal department.

Although the firm no longer trades in the town today, the business continues in Tenterden with Mr D.G. Knowles, the fourth generation running it.

The illustration shows the west side of Castle Street in the 1950s with the music, nursery furniture and electrical departments.

On the far left The Castle public house can be seen and next, a most popular shop, Jack Guy the pork butcher. Next is Burton's greengrocers and fruiterers whilst at No. 9 was 'The Paragon' confectioners and tobacconist and general stores. The proprietress then was Miss G.B. Harding. Photograph c. 1955.

KNOWLES OCCUPIED THE PREMISES at 106 High Street for over a century.

THREE OUTSTANDING PHOTOGRAPHS of Mr W. Richardson's fruit, flower and fishmongers shops. Mr Richardson had a great knowledge of the fish and fruit trade. He was editor of the Fish Trade's Gazette and wrote four large interesting illustrated books entitled *The Practical Fishmonger and Fruiterer*, which covered the history of the fishing industry up to 1915. He was also one-time President of Ashford Chamber of Commerce, Chairman of Ashford Urban District Council and, during World War I, Hon. Executive Officer to the Ashford Urban District Food Control Committee. The shop illustrated above was at 18 Bank Street on the corner of Bank Street and Tufton Street and remained in the same trade for many years. It was later occupied by Messrs W. Trice, another well-known Ashford firm. In 1916 Mr Richardson wrote 'we propose to open our new fish shop adjoining our fruit business at 18 Bank Street. This is for the convenience of our customers, who will be able to pass from one to another without waste of time.'

In conjunction with Mr Creery, Mr W. Richardson developed most of the Rising Road/Hillyfield estate off Jemmett Road in the 1920s (see p. 136). The development was managed by his son, Mr W.A. Richardson, who also made some of the bricks and blocks at the Beaver Farm Brickworks. The traditional name for a drying ground for the unfired bricks was a 'hackfield' and the modern estate now built on the ground is appropriately named Hackfield.

MR RICHARDSON'S ORIGINAL FISHMONGERS AND POULTERERS SHOP at 4 Bank Street, which he occupied in 1898, taking over the business from Elizabeth and Mary Hole. Along with Mr Burnage (p. 39), he was one of the first in Ashford to own a car. Mr W. Richardson at the wheel and his son, W.A. Richardson, standing alongside.

A MOST IMPRESSIVE and skilfully arranged window display at Mr Richardon's shop on the other side of the road at 9 Bank Street, now part of Messrs Hallett & Co. solicitors (p. 35).

IT WAS IN AROUND 1914 that Peter Crameri took over Messrs Paine, Smith & Co.'s catering establishment at 105 High Street, to open up his refreshment rooms. An Easter window display advertising hot cross buns.

THE BUSINESS was later taken over by the well-known Mr Bob Lightfoot, who acquired additional premises at 108 and 110 High Street. The elegant staircase leading to the first floor dining rooms is an excellent example of Shippam's (see p. 108) hardwood joinery.

THE DISTINCTIVE CURVED FRONTAGE of 108–110 High Street before it was taken over by Crameri's. Charles Clemetson was listed as a linen draper in the High Street as early as 1862. Crameri's finally closed in 1969 and the shop became the Record Corner and later Our Price Records. The beautiful staircase has been removed.

MIDDLE ROW, No. 1a, photographed in the last century. The premises were occupied by the old established firm of Thompson the printers, successors of Elliott & Son to whom the original W.J. Thompson was apprenticed in 1853. At the time, the craft of printing was coupled with gold and silversmiths' jewellery together with bookselling, etc.

MR W. JAMES THOMPSON continued the printing side of the business from premises next to The Swan public house in Tufton Street until his retirement in the 1980s. Mr Thompson is standing in front of his cases of type and letters are skilfully and speedily dropped into the composing stick. At the bottom of the photograph a poster can just be seen advertising a concert at Ashford Corn Exchange printed by Mr Thompson's grandfather a hundred years earlier in 1879.

GEERINGS OF ASHFORD. The firm was originally founded in 1903 by a local man, Walter Geering. He supplemented his South African War discharge gratuity with a loan of £100 from his wife-to-be Edith (who waited 7 years for their marriage) and set up a modest printing works in a small shed behind Albert Road. Within a year of starting business the firm expanded to a building on the corner of New Rents and Gilbert Road, shown above, later to become the Fabric Shop and subsequently the Singer Sewing Machine Shop.

The business was most successful and has grown over the years to a large organisation and is now the county's largest office equipment and business machine retailers.

GEERINGS' PREMISES at 83 High Street on the corner of High Street and Bank Street, were acquired in 1910. The shop was previously occupied by the Ashford photographers Messrs A.K. De'Ath.

GEERINGS ACQUIRED in 1919 the old firm of wholesale and retail newsagents Miller & Jarvis (previously Millers) at 80 High Street, where their main retail shop remains today. Extensive alterations were made in about 1930. Note on the left, the entrance to J. Broad's candle factory (see p. 71).

HEADLEY BROTHERS, THE PRINTERS, one of the town's major employers, was a business venture established in 1881 by two teenage brothers, sons of Henry Headley the grocer. In 1883 the brothers moved from a small room at their father's shop next door into 44 High Street, where the firm still has a shop today.

In the basement a newspaper printing machine was installed and in 1884 the brothers produced a weekly newspaper *The Kent County Examiner*. Published every Friday, priced 1*d.*, this was the forerunner of the *Kent Messenger*. The brothers also published other famous local publications, including *Headleys Guide to Ashford* and *Kent County Timetables*. The shop had the distinction of being the first in the town to generate and use electric light. In 1892 a purpose built printing works was constructed to the rear of 38 High Street (which in 1980 became the Downtown Diner). The photograph on p. 42 of Henry Headley's grocery shop at 46 High Street, shows, on the right, the truck that ran on rails for heavy goods to Headley Brothers' printing works.

Later a factory was built in Edinburgh Road, but was destroyed by fire in 1906.

AFTER THE FIRE new factories were built in Lower Queens Road. The illustration shows new machinery, run by an overhead pulley system, installed in temporary premises in Macc Lane before the new buildings were completed in 1907.

THE COMPOSING ROOM. On the left, with the waistcoat, is the Composing Room Foreman, William Cuckow, who worked with the company from 1888 to 1945.

THE FOUNDRY. George Foord pouring in 'hot metal' from a ladle. Mr Foord worked for the firm from 1900 until 1958.

KENT PAPER COMPANY celebrated its Golden Jubilee in 1987. The firm was founded by Ernest Baker and Frederick Norman, a member of the family of 'Norman Cycle' fame (see p. 82), originally operated from the old Drill Hall behind the Palace Cinema in Tufton Street. The illustration shows the Tufton Street premises, where printing was also carried on together with the making by hand of saddlebags for the cycle industry.

A SITE WAS ACQUIRED in 1948 in Canterbury Road, South Willesborough, which utilised wartime Nissen huts. Soon after the war the company was producing a million envelopes a week which were sent all over the country for Littlewoods Football Pools. By the 1970s envelope sales alone had reached 250 million per annum.

THE PREMISES OF JOHN BROAD the Ashford candlemaker on the corner of 24 Park Street and Edinburgh Road (now demolished). Mr Broad opened his business in Ashford at 5 Bank Street in 1862 and lived over his shop which, in the 1970s, became the Halifax Building Society. In the 1870s Mr Broad took up the Park Street premises. This excellent, although rather faded, photograph reveals that Mr Broad produced a number of different lines in candles including 'Ashford wax candles' and 'Broad's night lights'. Apart from the candle trade Mr Broad was also an oil and general merchant.

His tallow works in Park Street, behind Geerings' shop, (see p. 67) existed from at least 1862. The melting tallow caused a most disagreeable aroma and there were complaints to the Local Board as early as 1866.

John Broad himself was an impressive yet quiet figure who outlived three wives and died in 1916 at the age of 86. However, the executors of John Broad's estate continued the business until about 1922.

J.W. HALL & CO. Mr J.W. Hall was apprenticed as a blacksmith in Sandwich and same to Ashford towards the end of the last century where he lived in Christchurch Road. His speciality was supplying blacksmiths' sundries to the local smiths and farriers, both in the town and the rural areas, delivering the items himself.

As a young man, anxious not to miss a sale if the blacksmith was too busy, Mr Hall would often don a leather apron and help to shoe the horse, thus giving the blacksmith a little time to inspect his nails, steel and bar iron.

As the business became more successful Mr Hall moved to Queens Road. He retired in 1920 and his son George then took over and formed a partnership with Mr H. Thorn. Mr George Collins, originally a Manager, became Chairman of the company when Mr Thorn and Mr Hall died. As a young man Mr C.E.G. Dowsey joined the company as a ledger clerk and became Chairman when Mr Collins died.

Mr George Hall's son Thomas came into the business in 1943, starting as a clerk, and became Joint Managing Director with Mr E.A. Gilbert who started with the company in 1935.

In the late 1960s the firm took over the large Smiths' Crisps Factory in Carlton Road, off Godinton Road, for their main depot shop, offices and showroom. Most of the buildings they previously occupied in Tufton Street were demolished for office buildings and the new police station.

The Ironmonger's and Builder's Merchants business, which also incorporated Agricultural Supplies, continued in Carlton Road until 1980, and subsequently became UBM, although J.W. Hall & Co. continued Calor gas supplies nearby.

MR J.W. HALL, the founder of this old Ashford business, was also a keen bowls player.

THE DISTINCTIVE PREMISES of J.W. Hall & Company in Tufton Street, which were thought to have been used as stabling in Napoleonic times. The slaughterhouse used to be next door and it was not uncommon for the cattle to miss the door to the slaughterhouse and find their way into Hall's iron store.

PAINES OF HEMPSTED STREET. The boot and shoe trade has always been well represented in the town. Standing outside Reg Paine's shoe shop at 41 Hempsted Street just before the business closed in the 1970s are, from left to right, Ron Mason, Roy Barton, Paul Davis and Mr and Mrs Reg Paine. In the early days Mr Paine used to take wares out into the hop gardens to sell to the hop pickers.

EARLS OF HYTHE ROAD. Mr C.G. Earl, a saddler by trade, started business around 1910 at 32 Hythe Road in a small shed provided by the local shed builder, Mr Hide, nearby. The shed cost £6. 10*s.* complete with combustion stove. The business moved up the road to the existing premises at 74 Hythe Road in 1922 and the original £6. 10*s.* shed was still in use as a storeroom until 1988. The business is still run by the Earl family, now in its third generation.

THE CORN EXCHANGE was built in 1861 on the site of the old archery butts, opposite the cattle market. The sale of corn was once one of Ashford's important commodities.

THE SOUTHERN ELEVATION was extended in 1904 and the classical columns, which had the effect of supporting the original pediment, were removed.

APART FROM CORN DEALING the building, which could hold 1200 people, was a popular venue for dances, roller skating and political meetings. The illustration shows the building laid out for one of the regular trade exhibitions.

EVEN UNTIL THE LATE 1960s, when the building was demolished, the corn factors' stands were still in regular use.

THE TANNERS HOUSE. The ancient skill of tanning hides by the traditional method of using oak bark to produce tough high grade leather lasted until 1956, when the Ashford tannery was then the second largest oak bark tannery in England. The industry has its early origins in the town and had been on the same site since the sixteenth century at least. Shakespeare refers to Jack Cade as 'the tanner of Ashford'. Much of the Ashford leather was used in the shoe industry and, in those days, many of the British shoes made from Ashford leather were exported. The Tanners House is known as the Whist and has a most dignified Queen Anne facade, dated 1707, which conceals its earlier Elizabethan origins.

Most of the oak bark was obtained from the local oak woods in late spring and water was obtained from the nearby River Stour. The tanning process often took six months to complete.

Herbert Pulleston became Manager in 1934 and, on his death in 1941, was succeeded by his wife Mrs Pulleston, who later became secretary of Ashford Chamber of Trade.

In 1972 a number of the old tannery buildings, thought to have been built in the early 1700s, were demolished to create Tannery Lane which now passes within inches of the Whist.

GEORGE TUTT working on a hide on the beam. Tanning was particularly hard work and often involved rather offensive working conditions. After passing through the lime pits the rotting flesh had to be scraped from the hide – a wet, cold and evil-smelling task

THE BARK BARN. The Victorian Bark Barn, photographed just before the new Sorting Office was built. The barn is an extremely rare Victorian building which was used for storing the oak bark prior to grinding. The building is now 'listed' as being of 'special architectural and historic interest', but applications have been made for its removal.

HAYWARD'S GARAGE, NEW STREET. The firm was founded by Charles Hayward of Christchurch Road, who left his job as a wheelturner at Ashford Railway Works in 1889 and set up business as a bicycle manufacturer at 32 New Street. On the day of moving he arranged for the local children, and friends, to carry the component bicycle parts on a parade around the town, complete with a marching band.

Cycle production was quite considerable, some being exported until World War I, when the firm turned over to war work. The business then went on to general engineering and motor vehicle work through three generations of Haywards, Charles' son 'Charley' Hayward and his two sons, Charles and Gordon Hayward. The site was later occupied by Caffyn's.

In March 1943 the premises were hit by a 500kg. H.E. bomb and some fatalities occurred. The garage was rebuilt, expanded further and by 1950 had 6,000sq.ft. of workshop space.

The mock-Tudor New Inn can be seen on the right, which replaced an earlier pub of the same name.

A PRE-WAR PHOTOGRAPH of Hayward's New Street Garage. The original bicycle shop can just be seen on the extreme right. The site was sold to Caffyn's in 1967, who remained on the site until 1988.

MISS BUSS OF SMARDEN with one of the first ladies' bicycles with pneumatic tyres built by Charles Hayward. Photograph by A. De'Ath.

MR CHARLES HAYWARD on one of his early Ashford-made bicycles.

ANOTHER OF THE TOWN'S MAJOR EMPLOYERS was the Norman Cycle Works, founded originally in Castle Street by Charles Norman before World War I and followed by his brother, Fred. The illustration shows the large factory built in 1934 in Beaver Road and (inset top left) their premises in Victoria Road.

NORMANS were producing some 5,000 bicycles a week in the 1950s, together with 600 mopeds and 120 motor cycles. The illustration, from their 1960 catalogue, shows the competition model B2/C. One of their best known lines was the Norman Nippy – the 'up to the minute' moped.

BYBROOK, A RURAL SCENE, yet less than a mile from the town. In the centre is Bybrook House and on the left, a magnificent barn which, together with the water meadow, became Bybrook Barn Garden Centre in the early 1970s. At the height of the hop industry in the nineteenth century the cottages in the centre were converted into oasts, but the round hop drying kilns were demolished many years ago.

A CHERRY PICKING SCENE at Ball Lane, Kennington. With the bird scaring clappers on the right is Tom Howland. The birds are a menace at cherry picking time and bird scarers were employed, either with guns or clappers, to prevent the birds attacking the crop. This task would start early in the morning as soon as the birds were awake. Willow baskets were in great demand at that period and there were a number of basket-makers in Ashford, together with osier fields to provide the raw material.

ASHFORD HOPS. Hops have been grown around the area from the earliest days of hop growing in the sixteenth century until recent years and finally finished at Wye in 1986. The earliest printed book on the subject of hop culture entitled *A Perfite Platforme of a Hoppe Garden* was written by a local man, Sir Reynolde Scot of Smeeth in 1574, although he is better known for his other book *Discoverie of Witchcraft*. Hops from this part of East Kent usually achieve higher prices than those from the better known hop growing areas of the Weald. One local variety of hops was known as the 'Eastwell Golding'. The local labour was often not enough to harvest the crop in September and the coming of the railway coincided with the boom in the industry, so enabling Londoners to assist with the picking.

Above, Jennings' hop garden Canterbury Road, Kennington, *c.* 1947. In the centre, with the strings used for tying the hop pokes, is Gordon Stew. Behind him is the wagonner Harry Smith and also with strings, John Wynder. Dick Lilley (left) is tipping the contents of the 5 bushel hop talley basket into the poke held by Jim Wood. The tallyman in the white jacket in the foreground is Mr Watson.

In the nineteenth century hops were also grown at Repton, Willsborough, Godinton Park, Bybrook and Barrow Hill.

HOP GROWING IS A MOST LABOUR INTENSIVE INDUSTRY and it is said there is a job to be carried out in the hop gardens every day of the year. Overhead wirework maintenance and some methods of stringing required the skill of stilt-walking. Tony Atkins of Kennington, stilt-walking in Jennings' hop garden at Kennington in the 1950s.

ASHFORD WINDMILL, a smock mill, was originally built during the 1800s and was situated at Regents Place near the site of the present telephone exchange. In the 1870s Stephen Sharp was the miller who also had a shop in the High Street. The photograph shows the mill being dismantled in 1872 when it was bought by Mr Matcham of Throwley who moved it to Badlesmere.

KENNINGTON MILL. A rare photographic postcard of Kennington Mill dating from the period of World War I. The mill was considered unique as it could be powered by wind, steam and water, although the old chimney had been demolished by the time this photograph was taken.

WILLESBOROUGH WINDMILL probably replaced an earlier smock mill and was built by Messrs John Hill of New Street, the well known firm of Ashford Millwrights. It was made up in sectional construction at their North Street yard. One miller claimed that in winter he would have to ascend the shuttered sweeps from the timber staging to chip away the ice. The mill was photographed here in 1938 in which year additional electric power was introduced.

PLEDGES MILL. Henry Sturgess Pledge was a country miller from Barham who, in the 1880s, operated the mill at Kennington behind the Golden Ball. Mr Pledge realized that the old-fashioned mills could not compete with the Port Millers and so, in 1890, he built the sturdy mill along the railway line in Victoria Road. This enabled the firm to turn out high quality flour and to compete successfully in what was a most competitive market. The mill was further updated a number of times over the years but was sadly destroyed by fire in 1984.

THE ASHFORD KENTISH RAGSTONE QUARRIES. Kentish ragstone has been quarried in Kent since Roman times and by the medieval period ragstone quarrying was one of Kent's major rural industries. Its use ranged from cathedral building to cannon balls. There were many quarries in the Ashford area, particularly in the Great Chart area, and quarrying continued at Chilmington and Willesborough until quite recent times.

THERE ARE MANY EXAMPLES of Kentish ragstone work in the area and it was a favourite material for most of the local churches, farm buildings, and domestic buildings. There are some particularly fine examples at Great Chart.

The major use of the stone in more recent years was crushed to form roadstone, but some of the highest quality stone was reserved for masonry.

Both illustrations are from the Chart quarry at Chilmington.

THE SOUTH EASTERN RAILWAY COMPANY'S route to the channel ports was originally planned to go through Maidstone. The people of Maidstone objected, but the people of Ashford were much in favour. The line reached Ashford in 1842 and it was not until 1884 that the London, Chatham and Dover railway connected Ashford with Maidstone, thus making the station a five-way junction.

THE RAILWAY COMPANY bought 185 acres of farmland in 1846, at £115 per acre, to build the huge Railway Works – the largest employer the town had ever known. The Carriage and Wagon Department opened in 1850. The photograph (c. 1857) is by S. Barns, one of the early Ashford photographers.

ALTHOUGH THE MAJOR PART of the Railway Works has closed, both the clock tower and gatehouse (right) and the water tower (left) still survive today. To the right of the water tower, under which is a well, was the timber seasoning shed; this is now the BR Southern Region Wheelshop.

NEWTOWN WAS AN ALMOST SELF-CONTAINED COMMUNITY, planned and built by the Railway Company for housing its employees. Together with the houses, the Company built a public house, school, public baths and library. Over the years Newtown was extended, but in more recent years the area has been redeveloped and comparatively few of the original railwaymen's houses remain.

ASHFORD MARKET ON A BUSY TUESDAY in the 1950s. The town was granted the privilege of holding a market as early as 1243. The Elwick Road site was opened in 1856 and has become one of the largest markets in the country.

THE ASHFORD CATTLE MARKET COMPANY LIMITED is one of the oldest limited liability companies in the country. Apart from cattle, there are regular sheep, agricultural implement, antique, household effects and car sales throughout the year, although horned cattle, as seen above, are now something of a rarity.

THIS PHOTOGRAPH PRODADLY DATES FROM BEFORE THE TURN OF THE CENTURY. Sheep were then often driven on foot some distance from Romney Marsh and down from the hills, the wagon being the only other form of transport. In earlier days a speciality of the Ashford market was the local Sussex breed of cattle.

AN ILLUSTRATION FROM THE 1920s. Motor lorries have generally taken the place of farm wagons. Note the interesting telephone kiosk just in front of the market toll house. The trade bicycle in the foreground belongs to Miller & Jarvis, the stationers and booksellers.

THE STURDY, SLOW-MATURING BREED of Romney, or Kent, sheep is one of the most ancient breeds. Its very existence considerably helped the woollen industry of the area and both sheep rearing and fleece grading is a significant local industry. The illustration on the right shows washed fleeces being left to dry along the wall of Gregory & Prentis, wool merchant's store at the bottom of East Hill.

ONE OF THE BEST-KNOWN flock masters were the Strouts family from Singleton Manor, Great Chart, whose wool stapling business was orignally in New Street at the rear of Caffyn's Garage site. In 1911, they moved to East Hill. Those premises were demolished for the Ring Road, but new premises were built in 1966 on land previously used by Mummery, the nurseryman.

IN THE EARLY DAYS, wool was bought at a negotiated price per clip, irrespective of quality. The system caused dissatisfaction from the better producers and, shortly after World War I, the Kent Ram Breeders formed their own association, which became known as the Kent Woolgrowers. The company, together with Mr Strouts' own firm, now known as Gregory, Prentis & Green, deal with all the wool from Kent, Sussex and Surrey on behalf of the British Wool Marketing Board. David Briggs and Geoffrey Underdown grading fleeces.

SHEEP SALE, ASHFORD MARKET, July 1938. In 1856 the number of sheep and lambs sold was around 2,500 but, by the time the Cattle Market Company was celebrating it's centenary in 1956, the number had risen to nearly 130,000.

UNTIL THE SECOND WORLD WAR horses were still a common feature in Ashford. The town blacksmiths were situated in Park Street, St John's Lane, Wellesley Road and Hempsted Street, together with additional smiths in Kennington and Willesborough. Even in 1847, before the impact of the Railway Works and with a population of not much more than 3,000, the town itself supported at least five blacksmiths.

In 1907 the Ashford Horse Parade was revived. The illustration shows the 1909 procession in the upper High Street lead by Mr W. Winan's Russian Troika which was driven by Mr Stilwell and followed by Ashford Fire Brigade with the steamer and manual under Deputy Captain Jarvis. Master Clifford followed on a 'smart little pony'. Next came the private carriages, the job masters class, the farmers' wagons and vehicles and the St John's Ambulance twin horse van. When they eventually reached the Corn Exchange Mrs Laurence Hardy handed out the prizes, and was in turn accorded a hearty vote of thanks on the proposition of Dr Wilks.

THE TOWN BUS. A carefully posed photograph of the town bus in the High Street, just outside the premises now occupied by Woolworths. The smartly dressed and hatted gentlemen have probably hired the bus for an unrecorded celebration. c. 1902.

WORGERS DELIVERY VAN. A pair of neatly turned out horses with oiled hooves delivering animal feed by covered wagon. Worgers have been in the High Street for many years and finally closed in 1988. Earlier their corn, seed and fodder store was at 16 New Street where they also sold garden seeds, pet foods, etc.

THE LCD RAILWAY BLACKFRIARS GOODS DELIVERY VEHICLE photographed just above Nos. 1 and 3 Albert Road. Note the traditional homemade hessian-bibbed apron made from an old sack. The turned up denim jeans were probably an unusual garment in Ashford at that period.

THE CORNER OF ALBERT ROAD AND PARK ROAD. A team of 'four in line' heavy horses, complete with harness bells and pulling a Kent wagon, pose for the photographer.

LORD GEORGE SANGER'S circus procession, photographed around the turn of the century, proceeding down Bank Street. The theme of the display was 'The lion and lamb' – surely not a real lion!

ELWICK ROAD. Horse-drawn gigs and carts trot down the elegant lime tree shaded thoroughfare of Elwick Road, built in 1852 and now part of the Ring Road. The photograph is taken from the Station Road end of Elwick Road looking towards the Market.

WHEELWRIGHTING AND COACHBUILDING has been a particularly strong trade in Ashford for many decades and different firms specialised in various fields. For example, the speciality of Edgar Manser of Station Road was rather 'up-market' phaetons, whilst Marshall Brothers specialised in ambulance work. This is an illustration of Marshall's premises in Kings Parade, looking across to the High Street.

THE FIRM OF HEATHFIELD & SONS' main trade was agricultural carts and wagons, and they turned out thousands of quality wheeled vehicles. In 1915 the firm was producing 30cwt, 4-wheeled farm wagons for £20. Heathfields workshops were situated at the rear of 132 Godinton Road.

 One particularly interesting old Ashford firm was the British Wheel Works founded by Paul Headley, youngest son of Henry Headley the grocer, which grew to be the largest wheelwrighting firm in the country. The business was continued by his son, Mr E.B. Headley, and over the years the dedicated workforce produced wheels for fire engine ladders, farm wagons, gypsy caravans, Royal coaches, trade barrows, Council barrows, etc. By 1921 31,000 garden barrows alone had been produced.

A photograph of the staff of the British Wheel Works taken in 1964 the year before the firm closed.

Back Row L to R: Keith Harris, Mr Stanton, —, —, James Passmore, Martin Raune, Mick Godden, George March, Dave Smith, Alf Hills, Ernie Gower, Brian Coleman.

Second Row: Sue Rumble, Mrs Hemmings, Nancy Hemmings, Kit Bracket, Connie Slingby, Lucy Coleman, Christine Older, Margaret Judd, Margaret Haywood.

Third Row: Pat Carey, Joe Burden, Charlie Pay, Charlie Apps, Jack Tyler, Bertram Headley, Miss E. Smith, Pat Pentecost, Lesley Hyland, Jesse Pentecost, Joe Bennett.

Front Row: Terry Knight, Billy Gower, John Clark, Bob Bingham, John Sanders.

BRITISH WHEELWRIGHTS WORKSHOP at Mace Lane. The photograph was probably taken shortly after World War I. Motor wheels on left, bull-nosed farm cart wagons centre and English Warner pattern on right.

THE WOODEN WHEEL is still far from obsolete in Ashford, for much of the unique machinery from the British Wheelworks was taken over by Crofords, together with many of the skilled workforce. Retyring the Speaker's Coach in readiness for the 1977 Jubilee at Crofords. Bob Bingham knocks down the tyres, whilst Nicholas Gill cools the contracting metal.

THE ASHFORD LITTER, a wheeled stretcher, that was developed by two Ashford men, Sir John Furley, son of Robert Furley, and Paul Headley, at the British Wheelworks. One sad local use of these covered litters was that, at this period, things were so bad that suicide deaths were common on the Ashford and other railway lines and the covered litters were employed to carry back the victims.

NEIL ROBERTSON STRETCHERS. A photograph probably taken in World War I. The stretchers were made largely from split bamboo and rope and the making involved much hand work. Often the stitching was taken home to be done in the evening as piecework. Thousands were supplied to the St John Ambulance Brigade, Ministry of Supply and Coal Board, etc.

ASHFORD UNDERWEAR CO., manufacturers of woven underwear, trade stand at the 1911 Ashford Exhibition at the Corn Exchange. Skilled hands demonstrated hosiery-making and corset-making. The poster states that the goods are 'As cheap in price as those made in either Nottingham or Germany'.

THE COMPANY LATER CHANGED ITS NAME to Twixwol and the photograph shows the large factory in Birling Road, which later became Energen. The premises were bombed in the war causing loss of life and great damage.

TWO LOCAL BUSINESSMEN, Stanley Marsh and Frank Hayward, set up a small business in 1931 for the repair of Ford vehicles. They combined their names to call the firm Stanhay and, in 1933, sold the business to the agriculturist John Edgson-Wright. The firm bought the Frederick Clark premises (see p. 107) and rebuilt it in the grand popular style of the 1930s. The firm became agricultural engineers of national importance. The photograph shows Stanhay's premises, Elwick Road.

SWOFFER & CO.'S WAREHOUSE in Wolseley Road, the road that ran between Park Street and Albert Road. Huge quantities of bananas were imported 'green' and hung-up to ripen in the massive cellar. The ripening process was assisted by small, wall-mounted gas burners. The photograph is dated 24 November 1931.

THE WELL-KNOWN FIRM OF DRAKE AND FLETCHER, agricultural, electrical and general engineers, has been represented in Ashford since the 1920s when Joe Hooker set up the Ashford works in Godinton road. He took with him Frank Mercer and Bill Bailey, who had just left Frederick Clark's engineering works in Elwick Road after they had closed down (see p. 107). This interesting firm was founded in Maidstone over a century ago where, in 1885, Mr Drake perfected the 'Drake' oil engine, some of which continued working for 60 years. he also built a car. In 1957 the firm was granted a 'Royal Warrant' for supplying agricultural spraying machinery to the Queen.

The photograph shows the new workshop, built behind Godinton Road in 1946, and was probably taken in 1947. In the foreground Ernie Jones is dismantling the gearbox on a potato harvester, whilst on the right, Bill Stevens is working on a binder. In the left background is Bill Goldup and also in the background is Cyril Carter working on a David Brown tractor and Dave Balcombe working on a hop washer.

The two brand-new Bedford trucks and the Bedford van were brought down especially for the photograph.

The agricultural division is now run from Ashford and the fourth generation Fletcher is with the firm.

FREDERICK CLARK'S ENGINEERING WORKS, Elwick Road. A wonderful array of agricultural equipment is displayed outside the works. Although the firm were agricultural engineers specialising in farm equipment, there was still a good demand for hand tools in the area. Note the quantity of hayrakes and mower blades in anticipation of June haymaking and the various patterns of bill hooks and bagging hooks hanging up in the window. The firm was established in the early 1870s succeeding Foord & Co at the Elwick Iron Works near the market, as engineers, millwrights, boilermakers, with additional iron and brass foundries. Over the years it went on to electrical engineering, contracting for steam ploughing, thrashing and setting up dairies, etc. By 1903 they claimed the largest and most varied stock of agricultural implements in Kent. In the 1920s they manufactured a wide range of goods, such as saw benches, sack trollies, grindstones, wheelbarrows, horse hoes, etc, under their 'Elwick' trade mark. There were four forges, together with a room which supplied lighting for the Corn Exchange opposite.

This old established Ashford firm was bought by Stanhays who redeveloped the premises in the 1930s.

MR WILFRID SHIPPAM was the cousin of the Shippam of Shippam's potted meat fame of Chichester. The firm were builders of high repute and the photograph was probably taken prior to 1911, as by then Mr Shippam's house and yard was at 11 North Street. The premises were later taken over by C. Jenner & Sons. Evidently the carpenters had to pass Mr Shippam's window en route to the workshop – no chance of slipping in late in the mornings!

THE OLD ASHFORD FIRM of builders, Messrs Epps, dates back to 1841. The illustration shows their float just before the carnival celebrating George V's Coronation in 1911. Mr Charles Isaac Epps is standing in the foreground on the left. The theme of the float demonstrates the skills of the craftsmen employed by the firm – bricklayers, carpenters, monumental masons, etc.

THE PREMISES OF MESSRS J. WOOD, on the corner of Norwood Street and Queen Street, is still just recognisable by the building on the left, which became Norwood Street Garage (Automobile Engineers) in later years.

The firm was founded by James Wood in Norwood Street in 1863. It passed to his son, James Benjamin Wood and then to his grandson, Frank Cecil Wood, who retired in 1963 just 100 years after the firm was founded.

The photograph dates from 1894. In the centre of the group, to the right of the timber tug, is Mr J.B. Wood holding rolled plans, whilst to his left is Mr E.K. Chittenden, who later founded his own business with his builders yard in Magazine Road.

The original James Wood specialised in carpentry work, although the firm was also involved in large projects, such as building the Whitfeld Hall in Bank Street in 1873, a number of houses in South Ashford and the fine terrace known as Welldene Crescent in Canterbury Road opposite the cemetery.

In the 1930s it would appear that another speciality was plumbing work, for their advertisement of 1934 stated 'Sanitary work carried out on the latest scientific principles'.

Undertaking and coffin-making has traditionally been a builder's task and the undertaking business still continues under the name of Messrs F.C. Wood from 21 Tufton Street (where Mr J.B. Wood lived for many years), and is managed by Mr J.F. Moon.

THE OLD DRILL HALL in Norwood street was demolished to build the new Police Station. Standing in the centre between the bicycles is Frank Palmer the outfitter (see p. 58), who was a member of the Kent Cyclist Battalion. Photograph c. 1900.

THE NEW DRILL HALL was built next to the station master's house in Newtown Road in 1910 and many local TA Units were represented and stationed here. The building was used by the Post Office as a sorting office between 1976 and 1986.

EAST KENT IMPERIAL YEOMANRY OFFICERS QUARTERS at Barrow Hill. On the left is the Barrow Hill Farm oast house and, in the centre, the tall brick water tower erected in 1898 (now demolished) which formed a conspicuous landmark.

PARK ROAD looking towards Albert Road. Most of the buildings in Park Road have now been demolished and the road divided by the Ring Road. This is a postcard from World War I with soldiers posing for the photographer. The card was addressed to Mrs Will Bennett in Somerset and her son states on the back of the card 'This is some town!'

WORLD WAR I TANK No. 245 was presented to the town in 1919. On the evening of the presentation saving certificates were on sale and every purchaser had the opportunity of inspecting the tank interior.

Although it is now a much loved feature of 'Old Ashford' it has not always been popular. J. Ottoway wrote to the *Kentish Express* in 1921 suggesting that the Council 'transport from Victoria Park some of the thickly growing shrubs and plant them closely round the unsightly object'. The correspondent's suggestion gathered some support and sympathy.

The illustration shows St George's Square after the tank had been permanently positioned and surrounded with neat spiked railings. Later a seat was placed in front.

The tank still remains a prominent feature in the town and in 1987 a protective covering was built.

A RARE ILLUSTRATION of the tank, which had a maximum speed of 3.7 mph, crawling along the Lower High Street.

ASHFORD WAR MEMORIAL. It was not until the early summer of 1924 that the War Memorial was unveiled. It was designed by Mr E.A. Jackson and built by the local firm of Messrs C.I. Epps. Mr T.G. Kither was Chairman of the War Memorial Committee and Mr Herbert Lee and Mr Julius Kingsford were Secretaries. It was planned to complete the scheme by extending The Avenue down to Station Road.

Later, names were added after World War II.

LOOKING ALONG THE MEMORIAL GARDENS towards Church Road. Some residential houses can be seen where the Library now stands.

ASHFORD DURING THE SECOND WORLD WAR. There were 2869 air raid warnings in Ashford and at the beginning of the war the town was the reception area for London evacuees. Part of the Battle of Britain was fought over the town and this part of Kent became known as 'doodle-bug alley'.

The photograph shows a wartime scene at St John's Lane in February 1943. The scene is totally unrecognisable today although the lane maintains its original shape. The photograph is taken looking up this ancient lane from Station Road and the Baptist Church can just be seen on the right. The hand cart belonged to C.I. Epps the builders, whose premises were on the corner of Station Road and St John's Lane.

ONE PARTICULARLY TRAGIC BOMBING RAID resulted in the destruction of Snashalls Bakery in Kent Avenue. The baker was killed, together with his wife, son and two of his staff.

DEVASTATION AT NEWTOWN. The bombs were obviously intended for the Railway Works which kept going 24 hours a day during the war years. Earlier there was bomb damage at the Alfred Arms, but it was reputed that within a short while it was 'business at usual' with the pianist playing in the Clubroom.

THE COMPLETE DESTRUCTION of houses in the Birling Road area. The nearby Ashford Underwear factory (see p. 104) was also hit with resulting loss of life.

NEW STREET. Another photograph which is completely unrecognisable today. Bomb damage to both shops and houses.

THE ORIGINAL COTTAGE HOSPITAL was situated on the corner of Station Road and St John's Lane and was maintained, almost entirely, by voluntary contributions from the people of Ashford.

The Cottage Hospital, illustrated above, was on the corner of Hardinge Road and Wellesley Road. The fine brick and tile building was financed in 1878 by Mr W.P. Pomfret, the Ashford banker, as a memorial to his late wife and was built by the local firm of Messrs Giles & Giles of 76 New Street. The children's ward was added later.

With the increasing population of Ashford, even more space was required. In those days there were no public funds available and again the people of Ashford undertook to raise funds for a brand new hospital in Kings Avenue. The old Cottage Hospital was auctioned in 1933, together with its laundry, outbuildings and grounds. It was for a time the Inland Revenue office. The building has now been sub-divided to provide a number of individual office suites.

To the left of the iron railings, a footpath leads down to Lower Queens Road.

THE NEW ASHFORD HOSPITAL in Kings Avenue was completed in 1928. It is a most dignified building, designed in the classical style so popular at the time. The builders were Messrs Godden & Sons of Hamstreet, and the architect was Mr E.A. Jackson of Ashford, assisted by Mr T.W. Harrison.

THE THEN DUKE OF YORK, later King George VI, with the Duchess of York, now Queen Elizabeth the Queen Mother, laid the Foundation Stone on 20 October 1926. They also visited Ashford Railway Works on the same day.

ASHFORD IS JUSTLY PROUD of its Fire Brigade. The records date back to 1826 although some form of organised fire station was in existence from about 1814.

Early on the clumsy fire appliance was kept in the church porch. It had a lead tank, leather buckets and was strenuously dragged to the fire by ropes. By 1869 the Brigade had some 730ft. of serviceable hose. Full uniforms were introduced in 1867 and the felt helmets were replaced with smart brass helmets in 1887.

One of early fire stations was situated at the top of the town in Gravel Walk, but the access was rather difficult to negotiate and, in 1876, the fire station moved to New Street, where it remained until 1894 and then moved to Kings Parade.

This is a rather faded, but nevertheless interesting, illustration of the Kings Parade Fire Station before the advent of the motor engine. The horses were stabled at the Saracen's Head opposite. It is recorded that it took just three minutes from the alarm call to get the appliance out, horses harnessed up and ready for 'the off'.

AN UNUSUAL PHOTOGRAPH of the Brigade taking part in some celebration in Tufton Street. The photograph must have been taken from a high window in a Bank Street building. Note the 'three ball' pawnbrokers sign hanging from the building on the left, for many years trading as Herberts, successors to Blair Long, who were first referred to in the town in 1856.

THE OPENING of the King's Parade Fire Station in 1894. There were many guests from other Brigades. The Ashford firemen are, front left (sitting) with the long side-whiskers, ex-fireman E. Joy, and second from right (sitting) is Captain F.S. Hart. Far right, with top hat, is ex-fireman R. James and also on the right, holding on to the steamer, Mr W. Jarvis.

THE ASHFORD VOLUNTEER FIRE BRIGADE survived until 1942, when it became part of the National Fire Service. One of the last photographs taken of the Brigade, possibly at the beginning of the war, has many familiar Ashford names. Sitting front: (left to right) Frank Knock, Captain Harry Shorter, Verral Knowles. Second row: (left to right) Dick Castle, Bert Palmer, Philip Jordan, F. Smith, Bill Newton, Herbert Lee, Arthur Lyle, Sonny Hanson, F. Bignall. Third row: Charles Ford, Peter Waghorne, Frank Ruffle, Freddie Forsythe, Bob Lightfoot, Charlie Brand. Back: John Caves, F. Hogben.

HIGH STREET, Nos. 77 and 79. At just after midnight on the 25 May 1884 dogs barking alerted Mr Scott, the jeweller of 77 High Street, to the fire that had broken out on his premises. Mr Scott and his housekeeper escaped without injury but the building, whose shopfront was dated 1666, was destroyed. The property was rebuilt and later occupied by Achille Serre the laundry in the 1950s and by J. Grout & Son the Estate Agents after their Station Road premises were demolished in the 1970s.

FROM 3 JANUARY 1870 until the Tufton Street Post Office was built in 1921, the Post Office was situated at 2 Bank Street, as seen on the extreme right. The premises later became the National Provincial Bank.

THE POST OFFICE SORTING OFFICE had been in Elwick Road from about 1906 until 1976. The building was later demolished for road improvements.

THE TUFTON STREET HEAD POST OFFICE built of red brick and stone, was opened on 2 April 1921 at 2 o'clock by T.G. Kither JP, Chairman of the Urban District Council. Prior to the opening ceremony a 'roll of honour' tablet was unveiled on which was inscribed the names of the Ashford and District Post Office staff who served in the Great War.

CHRISTMAS PARCELS inside the old Sorting Office in 1954. Left to right: Len Stanley, Assistant Inspector, Ernie Wright, Jeff Leonard, Dave Cook and Norman Streeter. The new Sorting Office was opened in Station Road in 1986.

IT WAS NOT UNTIL AFTER THE WAR that the first motor cycles were used by the Post Office in Ashford. This photograph from that period shows the postmen smartly dressed in the heavier uniform. The wearing of hats was obligatory in those days. Left to right: J. Young, J. Coleman, Mark Gregory, Mr Tate, Dave Cook, P. Featherby, 'Young Paddy', Tony Osborn, R. Bridger (Inspector), J. Chittenden, A. Buckman, next unidentified, C. Higgins.

VICTORIA PARK GATES. The land to create Victoria Park was purchased in 1898 and skilfully laid out to create imposing ornamental shrubberies, shady tree-lined walks, shelter and a bandstand. The cast iron gates situated in Jemmett Road still survive, and were cast by Buglers the iron foundry located at the top of St John's Lane.

A SUMMER DONKEY RACE in Victoria Park. The photograph probably dates from the 1950s. The familiar face of Mr Joe Fagg MBE can be seen on the right.

THE BANDSTAND IN VICTORIA PARK attracted great crowds. Pledge's mill can be seen in the background.

ASHFORD
RAILWAY WORKS PRIZE BAND.
Winners of 2nd Prize, Reed Section (Open to Great Britain), Crystal Palace, 1908.

ASHFORD RAILWAY WORKS PRIZE BAND frequently played at the Victoria Park bandstand. By 1911 the Ashford Territorial Band was having even greater success for they had, for three years in succession, won the National Contest for Reed bands at the Crystal Palace.

THE MOST IMPRESSIVE FEATURE of Victoria Park and a favourite photographic subject is the Hubert Fountain. Bought by Ashford businessman George Harper from Olantigh House at Wye, he presented the fountain to the town in 1911.

THE BEAVER ROAD CINEMA was built by the local firm of D. Godden & Sons from Hamstreet in 1912. It was lavishly equipped and the furnishing was carried out by Lee & Sons of the High Street. The opening ceremony was performed by Mr G. Knowles, Chairman of the Urban District Council. The cheapest price for the back seats was 3*d.* (just over 1p). In its early days the picture house was packed to capacity in the evenings and sometimes hundreds of disappointed filmgoers were unable to gain admission.

ASHFORD PICTURE PALACE in Tufton Street was situated where Courts Furnishing shop now stands. In 1916 the circle prices were 1*s.* (5p) and 9*d.* (a little under 4p) and the pit 3*d.* (a little over 1p). The old Police Station can be seen just to the left.

Souvenir Programme

ODEON Theatre

THE ODEON, now the Top Rank centre, opened in 1936 with seating accommodation for 1,600. The interior decoration was designed to 'give life and warmth without departing from good taste and artistic simplicity'. At the time, the projection room was one of the most up-to-date in the country. The first film shown was the comedy *Strike Me Pink* starring Eddie Cantor.

THE EARLIEST RECORDS of the Scout Movement in Ashford have been lost, but the first Ashford Troup certainly dates back to before World War I. Well-known names connected with the Rover Movement were Mr L.B. Pitt and Major Chard. The photograph was taken near the market on the site where Great Mills Stores now stands. The Troup occupied the old NAAFI hut left over from World War I which was later removed to Victoria Road.

SCOUT PARADE passing down the bottom of Bank Street into Elwick Road near the Corn Exchange.

ASHFORD BOWLING CLUB was opened on the corner of Church Road and Vicarage Lane on the 12 May 1909 by J. Stirling Esq JP supported by members of the Hythe Corporation and the Ashford Urban District Council.

ASHFORD SWIMMING BATHS was one of the largest open-air baths in England and was most popular with Ashfordians. The water used to run into the baths straight from the river. The baths opened in 1867 and the Ashford Aquatic Fete was a very popular event in early days. The cup for 1868 still survives.

THE FIRST SENIOR FOOTBALL CLUB in Ashford started in the 1880s and was made up of players connected with the Railway Company. Another early team was the *Kentish Express* football club, made up mainly from the paper's employees. In 1891 the two clubs amalgamated and played their first game on the ground behind the Victoria Hotel in Beaver Road. Ashford United FC photographed for the 1906/7 season.

ASHFORD CRICKET CLUB PAVILION c. 1925. Cricket was originally played on a field where Kent and Sussex Avenues now stand. In the early days, because of transport difficulties, generally only those clubs close to each other were able to compete. Nevertheless, there was much interest and it was reported a century ago that 'almost every inhabitant of the town considered it his duty, as well as his pleasure, to attend matches'.

THE WARREN, a deer park in the seventeenth century, just over a mile to the west of the town, has been a popular beauty spot for years. It was purchased in 1925 from the Hothfield Estate by Arthur Davis, who presented the land to the town. Much of the timber was felled when the land was commandeered by the military who practised trench cutting here. This, however, is a nineteenth-century photograph.

ASHFORD'S WORKING MEN'S CLUB originally opened in Bank Street in 1922. In 1925 a new building (above) was erected in Station Road, with an office (now demolished) adjoining. Another branch was opened in 1934 in Beaver Road.

THE SOUTH SECONDARY SCHOOLS, South Ashford. The background shows Rising Road, Hillyfields and Hillbrow Road. When initially marketed in 1924 by Mr W. Richardson, the estate was considered to be the finest site in Ashford with its close proximity to Victoria Park. Each semi stood on a tenth of an acre of garden and further land was available at the modest price of 30s. (£1.50) per foot frontage.

ASHFORD GRAMMAR SCHOOL was endowed and founded by Sir Norton Knatchbull in 1636 and the first school building still stands in the churchyard. The later Grammar School in Hythe Road was built in 1880. It became part of the North Modern School and the new Grammar School was built in 1958 and officially opened by Lord and Lady Mountbatten.

CRUDEN HOUSE SCHOOL at 3 Wellesley Villas, 1 Wellesley Road, now on the corner of the Ring Road and Wellesley Road – a private school for girls and young ladies. The school was previously held in the Clergy House in the churchyard. The illustration dates from about 1912. The well-known Ashford *Kentish Express* artist Xavier Willis lived next door.

COUNTY SCHOOL FOR GIRLS which opened in 1907 was situated on the corner of Station Road and Dover Place, the site now occupied by Crouch's Garage. The fees in 1916 were £2. 7s. for those under twelve and £3. 1s. for those over twelve. The building later became the Ashford Labour Exchange.

THE NEW GIRLS COUNTY SCHOOL along the Maidstone Road was built in 1928 and was, in later years, renamed Highworth School.

ONE OF THE MOST PROLIFIC Ashford photographers was Mr Alaric Hawkins De'Ath, who came to Ashford in the 1890s. His Studio was at 32 Bank Street (later Corkers Wine Bar) and his retail shop was at 83 High Street (later Hepworths). The boldly painted sign 'The Studio' on the flank wall of 32 Bank Street, illustrated opposite, could still be discerned in the 1980s.

THE OTHER MAJOR COMPETING PHOTOGRAPHER in Ashford in the first half of this century was Hugh Penfold, who also started a business at 100 High Street in the 1890s and remained there until the 1940s. The shop later became Marcus Stores. Note the imitation plaster stonework over the facia board.

A SINGLE TRACK has been cleared down the High Street and the ruts in the snow are probably cart wheel marks. Snow from the pavement has been cleared, but the frozen pump appears to be almost inaccessible.

THIS DELIGHTFUL SNOW SCENE at East Hill could be on a Christmas card. The much photographed sixteenth-century cottage, occupied for years by the Mummerys the nurserymen, was demolished to provide a car-park for the East Hill School.

SNOW SCENES ARE A TEMPTING, yet difficult, subject for photographers. The central foreground figure helps to give depth to the photograph. The slow shutter speed blurs the action of the woman sweeping snow from the pavement on the right.

STURGES ROAD LOOKING TOWARDS SUSSEX AVENUE. Houses have now been built in the gaps on the right. The sign on the end house on the right is Phillips, the clay tobacco pipe-maker, who at one time also had another factory in New Street.

A FEATURE OF MANY OF THE PHOTOGRAPHS available from the early part of the century is the number of Ashford folk who turned out for celebrations. The population of the town in 1900 was only about 12,000. Here Bank Street is absolutely packed for an unrecorded celebration – a scene almost unimaginable today.

A CROWDED SCENE in the Lower High Street – another unknown event.

A PROCESSION IN LOWER BANK STREET (possibly 1918 peace celebration). In the front foreground is Goulden & Wind's music shop at 35 Bank Street (later to become Thompsons the printers, stationery shop), and next at 33, Stanley Marsh's 'Baby linen and ladies underwear' shop – Stanley Marsh being one of the founders of the original Stanhay firm.

ANOTHER PROCESSION PASSING THE CORN EXCHANGE along Queen Street and Bank Street. The band in the foreground precedes a contingent from 'Beaver Band of Hope'. Hardly discernible in the left-hand corner is O. Bechilli's handcart, selling hokey pokey ice-cream at a penny a lump.

HEADWEAR WAS CERTAINLY THE ORDER OF THE DAY in the early years of the century. Every person in the street, with the exception of those looking out of Masters the plumber's window, is smartly hatted with a wide variety of headwear. To the left of Masters shop in the background is W. & R. Fletcher the butchers, a trade that was to continue in the premises for many years, the later occupants being Messrs Dewhurst.

CROWDS GIVE WAY in the Lower High Street for the mounted cavalry. The photograph was taken from an upstairs window and looks over Buglers the ironmongers displaying their Royal Warrant. Just to the left of Alfred Wells (draper and milliner), is the passage which leads down to St John's Lane. Presumably the event is Edward VII's Coronation.

A PRE-1900 PHOTOGRAPH of the junction of Bank Street and the High Street. The occasion is unknown, but the illustration reveals considerable detail. The crowd seems to be remarkably well-dressed. The large corner building on the right was the old Ashford bank, founded by Messrs W & G. Jemmett as far back as 1791. This was taken over by Lloyds Bank in 1902, and later rebuilt by Godden, the Hamstreet builder. On the left is Mr Thomas Bear's hair cutting and shaving rooms which, with its later curved, semi-circular elevations, forms the west end of what we now know as King's Parade. In the centre is 75 High Street, William Taylor & Co. corn dealers, later Worgers. The building was once an inn named the Pied Bull. To the left of the building at 73 High Street is A.G. Austin's wine and spirit merchants shop, whilst to the right towards the bank is the Worlds Tea Company, grocers, later known as the World Stores.

BEAVER ROAD was an area that was prone to flooding. The main problem was that the capacity of Trumpet Bridge acted as a 'throttle'. The bridge was rebuilt in about 1970. Here horse-drawn traps seem to be making good progress along a flooded Beaver Road between Trumpet Bridge and Eastmead Avenue.

CATTLE BEING DRIVEN ALONG THE SAME FLOODED AREA. No. 34 Beaver Road can just be seen on the right-hand side, where a plaque proclaims that the famous conductor Sir Malcolm Sargent was born there. However, the published biographies state that Sir Malcolm was born elsewhere.

BRIDGE STREET, SOUTH ASHFORD, seemed to flood more than any other part of the town and many locals still remember the days when bread, milk and other provisions were sent up the road by boat. Here the delivery cart has a ladder on board to enable goods to be delivered through the front bedroom window.

ANOTHER FLOODED SCENE of the footpath from Elwick Road to Victoria Park. The row of houses to the left are in Christchurch Road, whilst the large houses in the centre are in Jemmett Road.

MANY OF ASHFORD'S PUBLIC HOUSES have been lost over the years – Coach and Horses, Wellington, Somerset Arms, Drum, Eight Bells, Freedom of Opinion to name but a few. Illustrated above is the Park Hotel, Wolseley Road, on the corner of Stone Street. The Victorian Public House was demolished in about 1980.

THE BRITISH FLAG, 21 Forge Lane, demolished for the Ring Road scheme, was one of the many public houses to bear a name with military connections. It was built in about 1860 on land previously occupied by part of the Workhouse until about 1840.

A VICTORIAN ILLUSTRATION of the Red Lion in North Street, which by 1903 had been renamed The Lord Roberts. The Red Lion has a history going back to at least the early 1700s, but was demolished in the 1970s for the new road system.

THE INN CAN BE SEEN ON THE RIGHT in the photograph, dating from the early 1970s. Dennes' shop can just be seen on the extreme right and to the left of the inn is W.H. Gibbs', whose other shop at 97–99 High Street was demolished for the Tufton Centre.

THE MARKET HOTEL opened around 1858, still survives on the corner of Bank Street and Godinton Road, so named to attract market business. However, it has been renamed in recent years 'The Wig and Gavel', presumably to tempt solicitors and auctioneers from their Bank Street offices.

THE GEORGE HOTEL, 68 High Street, is the town's oldest surviving inn. The front elevation dates from the eighteenth century, but part of the inn dates back to the fifteenth century. There was once thought to have been a right of way through the inn from the High Street to Park Street.

A DELIGHTFUL PHOTOGRAPH of Canterbury Road, looking towards the Cemetery from the bottom of North Street. Note the fine gas street light on the corner of Albert Road. The large house (which now leans a little) on the right on the corner of Hardinge Road was occupied by Thomas Sylvester, the dentist.

IN EARLIER DAYS, one of the most attractive routes out of the town was along Canterbury Road and down Gore Hill. Every building illustrated has now been demolished. The Gate House, leading to Bockhanger, can just be seen on the left. Many well-known Ashfordians lived in the fine houses on the right, such as Charles Igglesden of the *Kentish Express*, Mr J. Stirling and Mr R.E.L. Maunsell, the railway engineers, Mr Edbrooke the clothier, and Mr Pledge the miller.

GODINTON ROAD LOOKING WEST — a road which has suffered many traffic problems in post-war years. In the centre background on the left is 87 Godinton road; the name of J. Wood, one of the local carriers, is boldly painted on the side wall. Later the house was owned by another well-known Ashford character, Mr Jack Keefe, who had a fruit stall in the market for many years.

A SCENE TAKEN FURTHER ALONG the road but looking east towards the town.

HYTHE ROAD, a scene still readily recognisable. One of the block of properties with gables on the left became Mellin's Bakery in recent years. Next was Hanson's fish and chip shop, for a long time run by Mr Cohen. The fish and chip shop trade still continues.

HYTHE ROAD, just over the railway bridge. The pair of houses in the centre have been demolished and flats, known as Raglan Court, were built on the site. The distinctive ornate turret of Linden House, built in 1880 and one of the tallest houses in the town, can just be seen in the centre.

AN EARLY PHOTOGRAPH OF BEAVER ROAD. Christchurch Church can be seen on the right and the pasture land in the foreground was developed towards the end of the nineteenth century. Just to the left of the tree in the centre is the Locomotive Inn on the corner of Torrington Road.

PART OF KINGSNORTH ROAD, previously known as Millbank. The cottages illustrated are from 252 to 274 Kingsnorth Road and some are of Kentish ragstone construction concealed behind the rendering. The delightful lattice porches so popular, particularly in rural areas, around the turn of the century have long since gone and some of the Kent peg tiled roofs have been replaced with modern concrete tiles.

THE CROSSROADS AT BEAVER ROAD with Christchurch Road and Torrington Road. Gandy Brothers 'fancy shops and Post Office' stands on the right corner. Mr Gandy, the Postmaster, published a number of postcards of the area. The premises later became the well-stocked Beaver Road Ironmongers which closed down in 1988.

KINGSNORTH ROAD. The Beaver Inn can be seen in the background on the left. Until this point the road is known as Beaver Road then becomes Kingsnorth Road.

MANCHESTER HOUSE, 110 BEAVER ROAD, situated on the corner of Beaver Road and Christchurch Road. From the latter part of the nineteenth century the drapery business was run by Mr James Frederick Goffin, who later took his sons into partnership. From the 1930s through to the 1970s the trade continued with Mrs T.R. Hubbard and later Mrs G.C. Hubbard. In recent years the shop has become a Kentucky Fried Chicken outlet.

DENMARK ROAD taken from Upper Denmark Road near the Torrington Road crossroads, looking down to Lower Denmark Road. Once predominantly occupied by railwaymen, it was just a few minutes walk from the railway station and, by the Black Path, to the Railway Works. It was almost a self-contained street, with the United Methodist Chapel, and a number of shops including a drapers and a pub – The Denmark Arms.

SLINGSBYS STORES at 41–43 Upper Denmark Road on the corner of Whitfield Road. An excellent illustration rich in detail which reveals that apart from the grocery trade, Slingsbys also sold galvanised baths, buckets and wire netting. In the 1960s the shop was known as Equity Stores and since 1983 has been Glenda Chapman's 'Beehive Stores' selling flowers and 'collectables'.

HARDLY RECOGNISABLE TODAY is the Hythe Road Post Office, probably photographed just before the turn of the century. As well as the Post Office, Mr Salmon the proprietor's business was grocery, millers and corn factors. In more recent years the premises has been better known as Dickinsons do-it-yourself shop – Mr Terry Dickinson was well-known for his contribution and efforts in arranging Ashford Carnival.

No. 44 OSBORNE ROAD, WILLESBOROUGH – the shop on the corner of Osborne Road and Hunter Road. The business was run in the early years of the century by Mr A. Pope, grocer, tea dealer and baker. The old bakehouse and store can be seen at the rear. Note the unusual feature of the 'fishscale' Kent peg roof tiles.

ACKNOWLEDGEMENTS

It must be stated that this volume would not have been possible to produce without the valued help, kind co-operation and interest of so many individuals and businesses who have an interest in the town. Over the years they have given valuable time, patiently answered questions and collated information. Many of the illustrations are by courtesy of those who have let the compiler have access to their own collections. Special thanks to Bob and Jean Turner, Ronald Crosoer, Audrey Hughes, Peter Fairman, Robin Lightfoot, Ken Geering and to Arthur Coleman who took the trouble to photograph the town in that vulnerable period of the 1960s.

The compiler is also indebted to Arthur Ruderman who has carefully perused the draft manuscripts and made many helpful suggestions.

Acknowledgements and credits for both information and illustrations are as follows: Mrs E. Ayres, Miss J.E. Bailey, Tony Baker, Mrs M. Boxall, Mrs P. Brindley, Walter Briscall, Ken Carley, Glenda Chapman, Messrs Charter Consolidated plc, Miss J. Clark, Mrs L.A. Clark, Arthur Coleman, Adrian Coulling, Ted Craker, Messrs Crofords, H.J. Cook, Ronald Crosoer, Norman Crump, C.E.G. Dowsey, Messrs C.G. Earl, Messrs Epps, Peter Fairman, Joe Fagg MBE, Bill Gamsby, K.R. Geering, Messrs Geerings, J. Goodwin, Gregory Prentis & Green, Halifax Estate Agents, T. Hall, Roger Halls, Tom Harden, C. Hayward MBE, Messrs Hallett & Co., E.B. Headley, L.W. Headley, Headley Bros. Ltd., Messrs Healey & Baker, Eric & Joyce Heathfield, Miss E.M. Hole, F.R. Horton, Doug Hooker, Mrs A. Hughes, Mrs L. Humphreys, D. Ingram, *Kentish Express*, Kent Paper Co. Ltd., Kent Wool Growers, David Knowles, Norton Lee DSC, R. Lightfoot, E. Ledger, Geoff Leonard, H.J. Martin, Ron Mason, V.G. Matthews, J.F. Moon, E. Murrell, Neville Norman, A.E.W. Palmer, Ron Pemble, Messrs Photocraft, G.J. Playford, Messrs H.S. Pledge & Sons, Cyril Raynes, R.H. Rix, A. Ruderman, John Sanders, Ken Sellars, Miss D. Shilling, Alf Smith, South Eastern Newspapers, Gordon Stew, W. James Thompson, Mrs H. Todd, Bob & Jean Turner, C.T. Ward, J.C. Watson, Miss N. Wellard, Gordon Wright, Douglas Weaver and Weaver Bros.